THE FAMILY HISTORY
Record Book

Peter Dewar

PAVILION
PRODUCTIONS

ACKNOWLEDGEMENTS

The publishers would like to thank the following for permission to use
illustrations in this book.
Bridgeman Art Library: title page, pp. 7, 15, 23, 25, 41, 47; *Peter Dewar:* p. 35;
Fine Art Photographic: back cover, pp. 4-5, 9, 11, 13, 17, 19, 21, 27, 29, 31, 33,
37, 39, 43, 45; *National Gallery:* front cover

First published in 1991 by Pavilion Productions Ltd
A division of Pavilion Books Ltd
196 Shaftesbury Avenue, London WC2H 8JL
Copyright © Pavilion Productions Ltd 1991
Text Copyright © Peter Dewar
Designed by The Third Man Ltd
Picture research by Jane Ross
Typeset by Dorchester Typesetting Group Ltd
Printed and bound in Italy by LEGO
ISBN 1 85145 685 6

Front cover illustration: *Mr and Mrs Thomas Coltman* Joseph Wright of Derby
Back cover : *The Travelling Photographer* John P. Burr
Title page: *The coat of arms of the City of London*

INTRODUCTION

Two hundred and fifty years ago, Edmund Burke, the great Irish philosopher, said, 'People will not look forward to posterity, who never look backward to their ancestors.' Whether we like it or not, each and every one of us has a string of ancestors from whom we descend, and *The Family History Record Book* is designed to assemble and record information about our families in a sensible, interesting and logical way, which will also assist us in our researches, as well as preparing our families for posterity.

In fact, if one stops to think, each one of us has had two parents, four grandparents, eight great-grandparents, sixteen great-great-grandparents and so on. This means that in ten

generations (three hundred years) each one of us will have descended from no less than 2046 direct ancestors and from 1024 distinct lines, indicating that we all represent an enormous mixture of families and genes. In twenty generations (six hundred years) the figures are a staggering 2,097,150 ancestors descending from 1,048,576 distinct lines!

The Railway Station William Powell Frith

Of course, the custom and tradition is for us to pay special attention to our paternal line, for it is this that usually determines our surname at birth. Indeed, it is only this paternal line (through which the unique 'Y' genetic chromosome is transmitted) in which the same surname is used throughout the generations, being handed down from father to son, although there can be exceptions where the name has been changed or the mother's surname adopted (e.g. in cases of illegitimacy).

Nowadays, with increased leisure and wealth, coupled with the ever more impersonal and computerised world in which we live, it has given rise to an enormous upsurge of interest in family history, born out of nothing more than good old-fashioned curiosity to know one's roots and establish one's identity. Tracing one's own family history can be exceedingly interesting as well as the greatest of fun. It must never just be a collection of dry dates and facts and faceless names, for it is all about the lives of one's ancestors, their loves, exploits, their successes and failures and where and how they lived.

Indeed the roles of family historian and of the detective have much in common, for both must be able to spot and make use of every available clue. It is also true to say that family history is rather like a tapestry which should not

Un Coin de l'Omnibus Julie Delance-Feürgard

So much of what is
best in us is bound
up in our love of
family, that it
remains the measure
of our stability
because it measures
our sense of loyalty.
All other parts of
love or fear derive
from it and are
modelled upon it.
Hamiel Long

only be colourful in itself, but it is also the
product of the interaction of many different
coloured strands. It is for the collection of these
strands that *The Family History Record Book* has
been designed, in order to record and build up
this information gradually and logically, generation by generation and weave it into a tapestry.
The guide that follows will help to show you
how to set about this and where and to whom
you should turn for help. You will also need a
big lever-arch file for filing all the many
documents that you will accumulate in the
course of your researches, and these will need to
be cross-referenced to the appropriate entry in
The Family History Record Book.

In particular, the book is divided into
sections recording details of the husband's and

Emigration William Collins

wife's parents (two each), grandparents (four each) and great-grandparents (eight each); there are a further thirty pages both for the husband's and the wife's families, which can be used to take back further certain selected lines of descent. Notes explaining how to use these pages can be found on page 66. Initially, however, it is recommended that you should refer to pages 54–55 in order to familiarise yourself with the scope of *The Family History Record Book* and thereby plan your research to best effect.

GUIDE TO TRACING FAMILY HISTORY

The cardinal rule of genealogy is to start off from a known and established position, and work backwards painstakingly, generation by generation. Usually the best place to start is

A Village Wedding Anon.

Each generation imagines itself to be more intelligent than the one that went before it, and wiser than the one that comes after it.
George Orwell

with your own birth. Beforehand try to obtain as much information as possible about all aspects of your family and relatives from all living relations, especially parents, grand-parents, great-aunts and uncles etc. Write down meticulously whatever information you glean from them, together with the date and the name of the source. Most families accumulate family memorabilia – old photographs, letters, papers, newspaper cuttings – and some have family Bibles (in which dates of birth, marriage and death are often included); some may have family tombstones upon which many useful details may be recorded. All these can provide valuable clues for your search.

BIRTH CERTIFICATES

Probably, you will already know the place and date of your own birth and the name of your parents. The first step is to obtain a full birth certificate (if you do not already have one) which can be obtained from the registration authority of the country (or state in the USA) in which you were born (see the list of useful addresses). Nowadays, all countries have a

I am the family face;
Flesh perishes, I live on.
Thomas Hardy

Registering the Birth Ralph Hedley

system for the registration of births, marriages and deaths, the earliest of which started in England and Wales in 1837, followed by Scotland in 1855, and other countries rather later. The details given on a birth certificate will vary from country to country, but it should at least give the forenames and surname of the child, the names of the mother (including married name if applicable), the name of the father (if married or known), the date and place of the birth and certain other information besides. Birth certificates can usually be obtained by post or by making a personal search of the indices, which will identify the reference from which a certificate can be obtained. For particular details, however, you should consult the appropriate registration authority.

'Goodbye' on the Mersey James Jacques Joseph Tissot

MARRIAGE CERTIFICATES

Having obtained a birth certificate which shows the parents to have been married, it should then be possible to search backwards from that date of birth in the indices of marriages, in order to identify the marriage of the parents and obtain a copy of their marriage certificate. Apart from giving the full names and addresses and occupations of the parties, and the date and place of the marriage, it often gives their ages as well as the names and occupations of the fathers of both parties. From the ages, it is then possible to deduce the approximate year of birth, thus enabling you to make a search of the indices for the father's birth, and so on.

A Wedding Toast Erik Henningsen

Where does the family start? It starts with a young man falling in love with a girl. No superior alternative has yet been found.

Sir Winston Churchill

DEATH CERTIFICATES

In the same way, if the death of a person can be established and a death certificate obtained, the age at death will often be given, enabling a search of the index of births to be made.

Thus by using the statutory records of births, marriages and deaths, it is possible to trace back the direct lines for up to five generations in England and Wales, although less for other countries where the national registration started rather later.

By the Fireside William Kay Blacklock

CHURCH REGISTRATION

Before the advent of national registration, however, one is at the mercy of church records for baptisms (not births), marriages and burials (not deaths). This presupposes that one's ancestors were church-goers and members of an established church, for the records of other denominations can be much less complete (see the list of useful addresses).

These church records are sometimes to be found in the hands of the present incumbent of the parish concerned, or they may have been removed to a central repository, as happened in Scotland. In other countries, such as England and Wales, copies of many parish registers were also made for the local bishop, and many of these are now housed in the appropriate regional record offices. But practice and custom vary a good deal from country to country.

Without a family,
man, alone in the
world, trembles with
the cold.
André Maurois

Sunday School Joannes Fabri

CENSUS RETURNS

As the parish registers deal only with that particular parish, it is necessary for one to know which parish to search. In some countries this link can be forged by reference to the decennial census returns, which date effectively from 1841 in the United Kingdom, and purport to include the whole population, their entries being arranged geographically under their addresses. Most countries have a regular census, although many are subject to a rule of confidentiality prohibiting access for say 100 years. The census returns from the start of the system to a century ago can usually be inspected, and if armed with an address given on a birth, marriage, or death certificate, reference can be made to the nearest census return in the hope that the people were living there when the census was taken.

The availability and detail of census returns will vary from country to country, but in general terms they will normally indicate not only the names, occupations, and ages of all those living at an address, but crucially will also give the place in which each person had been born.

Home Again Henry Nelson O'Neil

THE MORMONS

The other link, thanks to the Church of Jesus Christ of the Latter Day Saints (Mormons), is through their transcription and computerised sorting and indexing of many parish baptismal and marriage registers. These are sorted, consolidated and arranged alphabetically by counties on microfiche and can be a tremendous help, although it has to be said that they are not complete and they do include many transcription errors. Copies of the *International Genealogical Index* are available locally on microfiche for consultation at various of their churches or at leading genealogical societies, libraries and record offices. The British census returns are also now being microfilmed by the Mormons. A list of searchers can be obtained from their headquarters in Salt Lake City, USA (see the list of useful addresses).

The Soldier's Return Charles J. Staniland

'I sometimes think of marrying old Maltravers,' said Mrs Beste-Chetwynde, 'only "Margot Maltravers" does sound a little too much, don't you think?'

Evelyn Waugh

PUBLIC RECORDS

In most countries there is a wide range of public records, including wills and administrations, taxation records, land records, personnel and other records of the civilian and military services (Army, Navy and Merchant Navy) and the professions (including clergy, the medical profession, legal profession), as well as trades and guilds (which often include apprenticeship records) and the records of ex-patriots overseas. There are also libraries specialising in particular areas, e.g. all regional and national newspapers since their foundation. All these can provide useful areas for more specialised research. Obviously, details will vary from one country to another, but the list of useful addresses gives the names and addresses of the major national repositories, which may in turn be able to guide you towards more particular or appropriate sources.

Off to the War Thomas Baker

REFERENCE BOOKS

Other useful sources of information in all countries include the many and varied reference books, including the *Almanach de Gotha*, *Burke's* and *Debrett's Peerages*, *Burke's Landed Gentry*, *Burke's Family Index*, *Who's Who*, *Who Was Who*, *The Social Registers*, *Walford's* and *Kelly's Handbooks* and *The Genealogist's Guide* by George W. Marshall (see Bibliography). Researchers may also consult lists of the Army, Navy, Air Force, Diplomatic Service, Law and the Bar Advocates, the *Medical Directory*, university and school records, and the registers of many different professions and organisations. Many of these, covering many different years, can be found at libraries, record offices and genealogical societies which often house unique collections of local family histories and records. There are many genealogical societies in each country or region, and there is also an increasing interest in local family history societies (with wider interests than purely genealogical details) and one-name societies (dealing only with the records of those with a particular surname), all of which can be of great assistance to the researcher.

Poverty and Wealth William Powell Frith

Each family, however modest its origin, possesses its own particular tale of the past, a tale which can bewitch us with as great a sense of insistent romance as can ever the tradition of kings.
Llewellyn Powys

WILLS

Another area of public records which can be of considerable use to the family historian is the collection of wills and letters of administration. These are sometimes housed nationally and sometimes regionally, dependent upon the administration of each country, and reference should be made to the national authorities for details of their scope and access arrangements. Wills can often contain useful genealogical information, such as names (of living and dead), relationships, addresses, references to heirlooms and properties. Indices to wills can sometimes be consulted, and the wills or letters of administration themselves can also be examined upon payment of a nominal fee. In some countries such as Scotland there are many printed indices to wills and letters of administration which have been published by record societies and which can be a tremendous help. Unfortunately too often there is no national index as such and it is necessary, therefore, to search through the regional indices.

Reading the Will Frederick Daniel Hardy

MIGRATION

The seventeenth to nineteenth centuries saw massive emigration from all European countries to the American continent, to southern Africa and to Australia and the Far East. They also saw much migration within Europe.

Both immigration and emigration records vary considerably from one country to another

and there are many useful and specialised books upon the subject. Inevitably, one will first be tackling the problem from the immigrant country and, with luck, may be led back to the port or country of embarkation through researching immigration and shipping records. But beware; many immigrants, in making a new start,

The Emigrants' Last Sight of Home Richard Redgrave

I can trace my ancestry back to a protoplasmal primordial atomic globule. Consequently, my family pride is something inconceivable. I can't help it. I was born sneering.

W.S. Gilbert

deliberately left few clues to their former lives.
Moreover, many foreign names were Anglicised
or Americanised or changed beyond recogni-
tion. In considering migration, it may also be
necessary to refer to the migration records of
many different countries, and not only those
which are English-speaking.

HERALDRY

Genealogy is very much intertwined with
heraldry, because coats of arms are passed down
from one generation to the next. There are only
four active and official heraldic administrations
currently operating: the College of Arms in
London (responsible for all aspects of English
and Welsh heraldry and for much of Ireland and
The Commonwealth, as well as for those of
English, Welsh, some Irish or Commonwealth
stock); the Chief Herald of Ireland in Dublin
(for those of Irish stock); the Lord Lyon King of
Arms in Edinburgh (responsible for all aspects
of Scottish heraldry as well as tartans and clans,
and all those of Scottish domicile and descent,
irrespective of where they may actually be
living); and in Spain the Cronista Rey de

The author's coat of arms showing within one shield three distinct lines of descent.

Armas in Madrid. If your family has been using a coat of arms, it might be worthwhile writing to the appropriate authority to see whether any family information is already on record, or if there is no appropriate authority, there are a number of societies which have taken over the records and vestiges of former European heraldic administrations.

PROFESSIONAL ASSISTANCE

The secret of genealogical research is that each fact as it is established should in turn provide a lead or clue towards establishing information about the next earlier generation. Even after reading all the books mentioned in the bibliography, however, there is likely to

The Young Mariner and his Sister Carl Bauerle.

come a time when one can go no further and is in need, therefore, of professional assistance. Sadly, there are all too many charlatans offering their services in this field and prospective clients are strongly advised to use only those who are properly qualified by examination and/or experience and who are a member of a properly accredited professional organisation (see the list of useful addresses). Either one can use a 'record searcher' to undertake a specific search, or one can entrust the research as a whole to a genealogist, who will then report on progress.

FURTHER READING

In so short an article, it is impossible to do justice to the wide range of records upon which the family historian can draw. It is important, therefore, that any researcher should consult some of the many family history publications that are available (see Bibliography), in each of which there is a wider bibliography for further reading.

'Where Next?' Edward Frederick Brewtnall

I christened her Maria del Sol, because she was my first child and I dedicated her to the glorious sun of Castile: but her mother calls her Sally, and her brother Pudding-Face.
W. Somerset Maugham

SOCIETIES

It is important too that family historians should become members of relevant genealogical, family history or one-name societies, not only in order to make use of their facilities and the fruits of their researches, but also so as to share their experiences with other members from whom there is always much to learn. The most important societies are listed in the list of useful addresses, and most have collections of unique genealogical material and local and national books. They will also put enquirers in touch with more local societies. Some also operate a postal service for researchers.

Whatever library or record office or organisation you may wish to visit, however, you would be well advised to telephone them in advance of your visit, to find out what arrangements are required for your research.

'Goodnight' Thomas Webster

One of the deepest impulses in man is the impulse to record, to scratch a drawing on the tusk or keep a diary, to collect sagas and heap cairns. This instinct as to the enduring value of the past is, one might say, the very basis of civilization.
John Jay Chapman

Researching your family history will take much time and can be frustrating, but it is also addictive and the greatest of fun. If records are available you should be able to make useful progress, even after having gone down some blind alleys. However much or little you are able to discover, it will be of extraordinary interest to your own family and to your descendants in the future. Indeed, by recording your research in *The Family History Record Book* you will have left your own small mark on history, for the benefit of generations yet to come.

Reading a Letter Epp Rudolf

USEFUL ADDRESSES

For the addresses of principal libraries, record offices and repositories around the world, consult the *International Directory of Archives,* published in the periodical *Archivum* (Vol 5 22-23, 1972-3).

ENGLAND AND WALES

Most counties have a County Record Office, but see telephone directories for addresses.

The General Register Office (Births, Marriages and Deaths), St Catherine's House, 10 Kingsway, London WC2B 6JB

The Public Record Office (Census Section), Portugal Street, London WC2A 3PH

The Public Record Office (Medieval, Legal, Probate and Non-Conformist Records), Chancery Lane, London WC2A 1LR

The Public Record Office (Army, Navy, Foreign and Home Office Records, Board of Trade and Inland Revenue Papers), Ruskin Avenue, Kew, Richmond, Surrey TW9 4DU

The Principal Probate Registry (Wills and Letters of Administration), Somerset House, Strand, London WC2R 1LP

The College of Arms, Queen Victoria Street, London EC4V 4BT

The British Library, The British Museum, Great Russell Street, London WC1B 3DG

The British Library Newspaper Library, Colindale Avenue, London NW9 5HE

The National Library of Wales, Department of Manuscripts and Records, Aberystwyth, Dyfed SY23 3BU

Guildhall Library (City of London), Aldermanbury, London EC2P 2EJ

India Office Library and Records, 197 Blackfriars Road, London SE1 8NG

The Society of Genealogists, 14 Charterhouse Buildings, Goswell Road, London EC1 7BA

The Association of Genealogists and Record Agents, c/o Mrs Pat Bunner, 15 Dover Close, Hill House, Fareham, Hants PO14 3SU

The Institute of Heraldic and Genealogical Studies, Northgate, Canterbury, Kent CT1 1BA

The Federation of Family History Societies, The Administrator, 31 Seven Star Road, Solihull, West Midlands B91 2BZ

The Heraldry Society, 44-45 Museum Street, London WC1A 1LH

The Society for Army Historical Research, c/o The Library, Old War Office Building, London SW1A 2HB

The Military Historical Society, Duke of York's Headquarters, London SW3 4SG (Postal enquiries only)

The National Army Museum, Royal Hospital Road, London SW3 4HT

The National Maritime Museum, Park Row, London SE10 9NF

Packing a Trunk Frank Hobden

The novelties of one generation are only the resuscitated fashions of the generation before last.
George Bernard Shaw

Navy Records Society, Royal Navy College, London SE10 9NF

Imperial War Museum, Lambeth Road, London SE1 6HZ

The Jewish Museum and Central Library, Woburn House, Upper Woburn Place, London WC1H 0EP

The Library of the Society of Friends (Quakers), Friends' House, Euston Road, London NW1 3BJ

The Catholic Record Society, 114 Mount Street, London W1Y 6AH

The Archivist, Archdiocese of Westminster, 16A Abingdon Road, London W8 6AF

The Church of Jesus Christ of the Latter Day Saints (Mormons), London Genealogical Library, 64 Exhibition Road, London SW7 2PA

Doctor Williams' Library (Non-Conformists), 14 Gordon Square, London WC1H 0AG

SCOTLAND

The General Register Office (Births, Marriages, Deaths and Parish Registers), New Register House, Edinburgh, EH1 3YT

The Scottish Record Office (Land Registry), HM General Register House, Princes Street, Edinburgh EH1 3YY

The Court of the Lord Lyon King of Arms, HM New Register House, Edinburgh EH1 3YT

The National Library of Scotland, George IV Bridge, Edinburgh EH1 1EW

Scots Ancestry Research Society, 3 Albany Street, Edinburgh EH1 3PY

The Association of Scottish Genealogists and Record Agents, PO Box 174, Edinburgh EH3 5QZ

IRELAND

The General Register Office, 8-11 Lombard East, Dublin 2

The General Register Office (Births, Marriages and Deaths), 49-55 Chichester Street, Belfast BT1 4HL

The Public Record Office, Four Courts, Dublin 7

The Public Record Office of Northern Ireland, 66 Balmoral Avenue, Belfast BT9 6NY

The Genealogical Office, Dublin Castle, Kildare Street, Dublin 2

The National Library of Ireland, Kildare Street, Dublin 2

The Irish Genealogical Research Society, c/o Challoner Club, 61 Pont Street, London SW1X 0BG

AUSTRALIA

The Registrar of Births, Deaths and Marriages, Prince Albert Road, Sydney, New South Wales 2000

The Principal Register, GPO Box 1351 H, Adelaide, South Australia 50001

The Bayswater Omnibus George William Joy

The Registrar General, Oakleigh Building, 22 St George's Terrace, Perth, Western Australia 6000

The Public Record Office, 328 Swanston Street, Melbourne, Victoria 3000

The Queensland State Archivist, 162 Annerley Road, Dutton Park, Queensland 4102

The Mitchell Library, Macquarie Street, Sydney, New South Wales 2000

The Society of Australian Genealogists, Richmond Villa, 120 Kent Street, Sydney, New South Wales 2000

The Australasian Federation of Family History Organisations, PO Box 30, Blackhouse, Victoria 3130

1788-1820 Pioneer Association, 44 Margaret Street, Sydney, New South Wales 2000

CANADA

National Archives of Canada, 395 Wellington Street, Ottawa, Ontario, KIA ON4

The Genealogical Research Library Inc., 86 Gerrard East, Toronto, Ontario M5B 2J1

The Ontario Genealogical Society, 40 Orchard View, Boulevard #253, Toronto, Ontario M4R 1BN

The Family History Association of Canada, PO Box 398, West Vancouver, British Columbia V7

Heraldry Society of Canada, PO Box 8467, Station T, Ottawa, Ontario, K1

NEW ZEALAND

The Registrar General's Office, PO Box 5024, Lambton Quay, Wellington

The Commonwealth Heraldry Board, PO Box 23-056, Papatoetoe, Auckland

The National Library of New Zealand, Auckland

The Armorial and Genealogical Institute of New Zealand, PO Box 13301, Armagh, Christchurch

The New Zealand Society of Genealogists, PO Box 8795, Symonds Street, Auckland

The New Zealand Founders' Society, 90 The Terrace, Wellington

SOUTH AFRICA

The State Archives and Heraldic Services, Private Bag 236, INA Building, Schoeman Street, 0001 Pretoria

The Institute for Genealogical Research, Human Sciences Research Council, Private Bag X41, 0001 Pretoria

The South African Library, Queen Victoria Street, Cape Town 8001

The Genealogical Society of South Africa, PO Box 3057, Coetzernburg 7602

The Heraldry Society of Southern Africa, PO Box 4839, Cape Town 8000

THE UNITED STATES OF AMERICA

The United States have a great number of public record offices and genealogical societies. The addresses of those which deal with your particular area should be obtained from the following:

The National Archives, 8th and Pennsylvania Avenue, Washington DC 20408

The Library of Congress, 10 First Street SE, Washington DC 20540

The Genealogical Library of the Church of Jesus Christ of Latter-Day Saints, 35 North West Temple Street, Salt Lake City, Utah 84150 (includes the International Genealogical Index)

The American College of Arms, Heralds Mews on Longdock, Harbourmaster Buildings, Baltimore, Maryland 21202

The National Genealogical Society, 4527 17th Street North, Arlington, Virginia 22207

The Federation of Genealogical Societies, PO Box 220, Davenport, Iowa 52805

The International Society for British Genealogy and Family History, PO Box 20425, Cleveland, Ohio 44120

The New York Genealogical and Biographical Society, 122 East 58th Street, New York, New York 10022

EUROPE

Heraldisch-Genealogisch Gesellschaft 'Adler', Haarhof 4a, A-1010 Vienna, Austria

L'Office Généalogique et Heraldique de Belgique, Musées Royaux d'Art et d'Histoire, 10 Avenue des Nerviens, B-1040 Brussels, Belgium

The International Academy of Heraldry, Rue Martin Lindekens 57, B-1150 Brussels, Belgium

Samfundet for Dansk Genealogi og Personalhistorie, Grysgardsvej 2, DK2400 Kobenhavn NV, Denmark

Centre d'Entre Aide Généalogique, 69 rue du Cardinal Lemoine, F-75005 Paris, France

Deutsche Arbeitsgemeinschaft, Genealogischer Verbande e. V., Schlossstrasse 12, D-5040 Bruhl, West Germany

Istituto Storice Famiglie Italiane, Via Cavour 31, 50129 Firenze, Italy

Central Bureau voor Genealogie,
Postbus 11755, NL-2502-ATs
Gravenhage, The Netherlands

Norsk Slekthistorisk Forening, Ovre
Slottsgate 17, Oslo 1, Norway

The Polish Genealogical Society, Inc.
984 North Milwaukee Avenue, Chicago,
Illinois 60622, USA

Arquiva Naccional da Torre Tonba,
Lisbon, Portugal

Cronista Rey de Armas, Ministry of
Justice, Madrid, Spain

Sociedad Toledana de Estudios
Heraldicos y Genealogicos, Apartado de
Concos 373, Toledo, Spain

Genealogiska Foreningen, Box 2029,
S-1031.1 Stockholm, Sweden

Schweizerische Gesellschaft für
Familienforschung, Eichholzstrasse 19,
CH-8706 Feldmeilen, Switzerland

SELECT BIBLIOGRAPHY

Major publishers of books on genealogy
include Phillimore and Co. Ltd,
Shopwyke Hall, Chichester, Sussex,
England, and the Genealogical
Publishing Co. Inc., Baltimore,
Maryland, USA, who will send a
catalogue on request.

Andereck, P. and Pence, R. *Computer genealogy: a guide to research through high technology* (1985)

Baxter, Angus *In Search of your European Roots* (1986)

Beard, T.F. and Demong, D. *How to find your family roots* (1977)

Begley, D.F. *Handbook of Irish Genealogy* (1980)

Currer-Briggs, Noel *Worldwide Family History* (1982)

Earle, A. and Cerny, J. (eds.) *The Source: a guidebook of American genealogy* (1984)

Filby, P.W. and Meyer, M.K. *Passenger and Immigration Lists Bibliography 1538-1900* (1988)

FitzHugh, Terrick U.H. *The Dictionary of Genealogy* (1985)

Galbraith, U.H. *An introduction to the Use of Public Records* (1934)

Gambier, R. and Currer-Briggs, N. *Debrett's Family Historian* (1981)

Hamilton-Edwards, Gerald *In Search of Scottish Ancestry* (1980)

Hawkings, D.T. *Bound for Australia* (1986)

Kemp, Thomas J. *Vital Records* (1988)

Lombard, R.T.J. *Handbook for Genealogical Research in South Africa* (1984)

Marshall, George W. *The Genealogist's Guide* (1967)

Willis, A.J. *Genealogy for Beginners* (1976)

THE
FAMILY TREE
— OF —

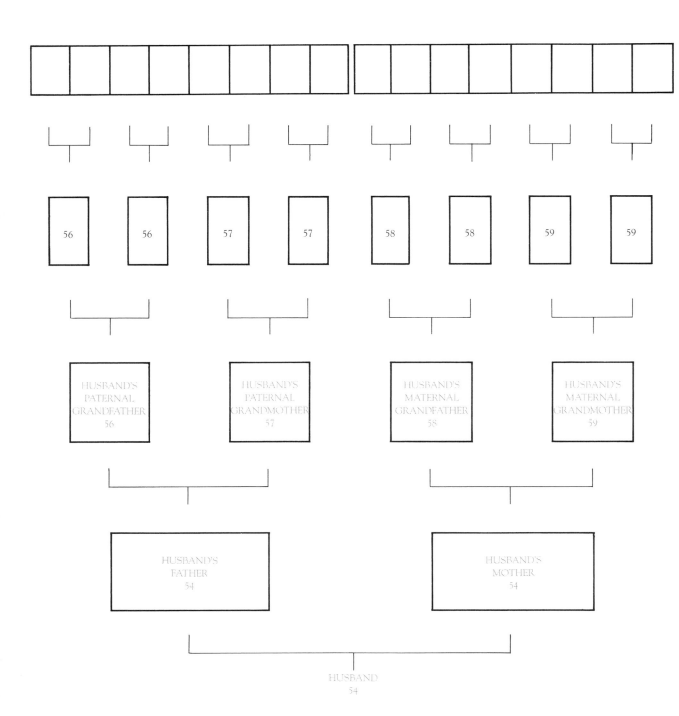

56   56   57   57   58   58   59   59

HUSBAND'S
PATERNAL
GRANDFATHER
56

HUSBAND'S
PATERNAL
GRANDMOTHER
57

HUSBAND'S
MATERNAL
GRANDFATHER
58

HUSBAND'S
MATERNAL
GRANDMOTHER
59

HUSBAND'S
FATHER
54

HUSBAND'S
MOTHER
54

HUSBAND
54

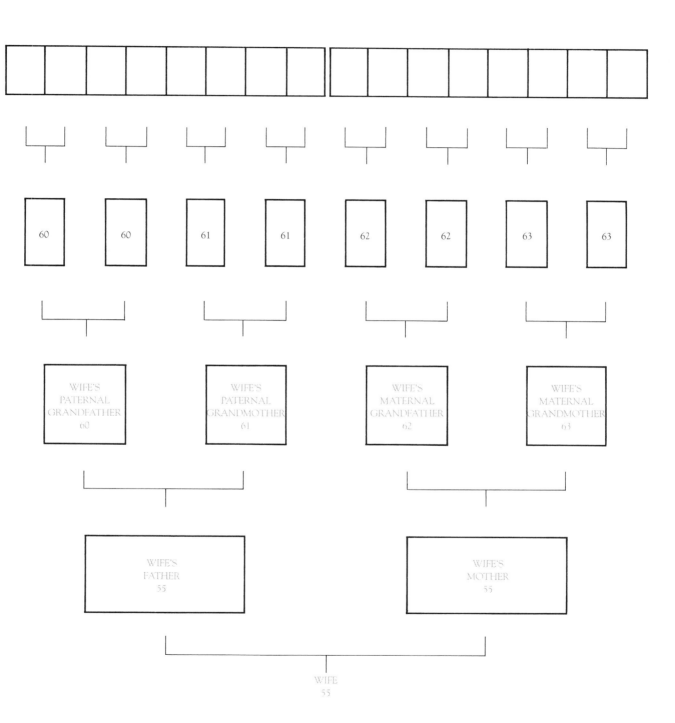

56/7 ↑

Name ....

Born on .... at ....

Educated ....

....

Qualifications ....

....

Career ....

....

Achievements ....

....

Addresses ....

....

Died on .... at ....

Buried on .... at ....

58/9 ↑

Name ....

Born on .... at ....

Educated ....

....

Achievements/career ....

....

Married on .... at ....

....

Other children .... Born ....

.... Born ....

.... Born ....

.... Born ....

Died on .... at ....

Buried on .... at ....

2 ◇ HUSBAND'S FATHER

HUSBAND'S MOTHER ◇ 2

Name ....

Born on .... at ....

Educated ....

....

Qualifications ....

....

Career ....

....

Achievements ....

....

Addresses ....

....

Died on .... at ....

Buried on .... at ....

1 ◇ HUSBAND

60/1

Name ....

Born on .... **at** ....

Educated ....

....

Qualifications ....

....

Career ....

....

Achievements ....

....

Addresses ....

....

Died on .... **at** ....

Buried on .... **at** ....

62/31

Name ....

Born on .... **at** ....

Educated ....

....

Achievements/career ....

....

Married on .... **at** ....

Other children .... **Born** ....

.... **Born** ....

.... **Born** ....

.... **Born** ....

Died on .... **at** ....

Buried on .... **at** ....

⟨2⟩   WIFE'S FATHER   WIFE'S MOTHER   ⟨2⟩

Name ....

Born on .... **at** ....

Educated ....

....

Qualifications ....

....

Career ....

....

Achievements ....

....

Addresses ....

....

Died on .... **at** ....

Buried on .... **at** ....

WIFE ⟨1⟩

Name ....

Born on .... at ....

Educated ....

Qualifications ....

....

Career ....

....

Achievements ....

....

Addresses ....

....

Died on .... at ....

Buried on .... at ....

HUSBAND'S PATERNAL
PATERNAL GREAT-GRANDFATHER

4

Name ....

Born on .... at ....

Educated ....

....

Achievements/career ....

....

Married on .... at ....

Other children .... Born ....

.... Born ....

.... Born ....

.... Born ....

Died on .... at ....

Buried on .... at ....

HUSBAND'S PATERNAL
PATERNAL GREAT-GRANDMOTHER

4

54

Name ....

Born on .... at ....

Educated ....

....

Qualifications ....

....

Career ....

....

Achievements ....

....

Addresses ....

....

Died on .... at ....

Buried on .... at ....

HUSBAND'S
PATERNAL GRANDFATHER

3

Name ....

Born on .... at ....

Educated ....

....

Qualifications ....

....

Career ....

....

Achievements ....

....

Addresses ....

....

Died on .... at ....

Buried on .... at ....

H U S B A N D ' S   P A T E R N A L
M A T E R N A L   G R E A T - G R A N D F A T H E R

Name ....

Born on .... at ....

Educated ....

....

Achievements/career ....

....

Married on .... at ....

Other children .... Born ....

.... Born ....

.... Born ....

.... Born ....

Died on .... at ....

Buried on .... at ....

H U S B A N D ' S   P A T E R N A L
M A T E R N A L   G R E A T - G R A N D M O T H E R

Name ....

Born on .... at ....

Educated ....

....

Qualifications ....

....

Career ....

....

Achievements ....

....

Addresses ....

....

Died on .... at ....

Buried on .... at ....

H U S B A N D ' S
P A T E R N A L   G R A N D M O T H E R

Name ....

Born on .... at ....

Educated ....

Qualifications ....

Career ....

Achievements ....

Addresses ....

Died on .... at ....

Buried on .... at ....

HUSBAND'S MATERNAL
PATERNAL GREAT-GRANDFATHER

Name ....

Born on .... at ....

Educated ....

Achievements/career ....

Married on .... at ....

Other children .... Born ....

.... Born ....

.... Born ....

.... Born ....

Died on .... at ....

Buried on .... at ....

HUSBAND'S MATERNAL
PATERNAL GREAT-GRANDMOTHER

Name ....

Born on .... at ....

Educated ....

Qualifications ....

Career ....

Achievements ....

Addresses ....

Died on .... at ....

Buried on .... at ....

HUSBAND'S
MATERNAL GRANDFATHER

58

Name ....

Born on .... **at** ....

Educated ....

....

Qualifications ....

....

Career ....

....

Achievements ....

....

Addresses ....

....

Died on .... **at** ....

Buried on .... **at** ....

HUSBAND'S MATERNAL
MATERNAL GREAT-GRANDFATHER

Name ....

Born on .... **at** ....

Educated ....

....

Achievements/career ....

....

Married on .... **at** ....

....

Other children .... **Born** ......

.... **Born** ......

.... **Born** ......

.... **Born** ......

Died on .... **at** ....

Buried on .... **at** ....

HUSBAND'S MATERNAL
MATERNAL GREAT-GRANDMOTHER   4

Name   54

Born on .... **at** ....

Educated ....

....

Qualifications ....

....

Career ....

....

Achievements ....

....

Addresses ....

....

Died on .... **at** ....

Buried on .... **at** ....

HUSBAND'S
MATERNAL GRANDMOTHER   3

Name ....

Born on .... **at** ....

Educated ....

....

Qualifications ....

....

Career ....

....

Achievements ....

....

Addresses ....

....

Died on .... **at** ....

Buried on .... **at** ....

Name ....

Born on .... **at** ....

Educated ....

....

Achievements/career ....

....

Married on .... **at** ....

....

Other children .... **Born** ....

.... **Born** ....

.... **Born** ....

.... **Born** ....

Died on .... **at** ....

Buried on .... **at** ....

WIFE'S PATERNAL
4 PATERNAL GREAT-GRANDFATHER

WIFE'S PATERNAL
PATERNAL GREAT-GRANDMOTHER 4

55

Name ....

Born on .... **at** ....

Educated ....

....

Qualifications ....

....

Career ....

....

Achievements ....

....

Addresses ....

....

Died on .... **at** ....

Buried on .... **at** ....

WIFE'S
3 PATERNAL GRANDFATHER

Name ....

Born on .... **at** ....

Educated ....

....

Qualifications ....

....

Career ....

....

Achievements ....

....

Addresses ....

....

Died on .... **at** ....

Buried on .... **at** ....

4

WIFE'S PATERNAL
MATERNAL GREAT-GRANDFATHER

Name ....

Born on .... **at** ....

Educated ....

....

Achievements/career ....

....

Married on .... **at** ....

Other children .... **Born** ....

.... **Born** ....

.... **Born** ....

.... **Born** ....

Died on .... **at** ....

Buried on .... **at** ....

WIFE'S PATERNAL
MATERNAL GREAT-GRANDMOTHER

4

Name ....

Born on .... **at** ....

Educated ....

....

Qualifications ....

....

Career ....

....

Achievements ....

....

Addresses ....

....

Died on .... **at** ....

Buried on .... **at** ....

55

WIFE'S
PATERNAL GRANDMOTHER

3

Name ....

Born on .... **at** ....

Educated ....

....

Qualifications ....

....

Career ....

....

Achievements ....

....

Addresses ....

....

Died on .... **at** ....

Buried on .... **at** ....

4 WIFE'S MATERNAL
PATERNAL GREAT-GRANDFATHER

Name ....

Born on .... **at** ....

Educated ....

....

Achievements/career ....

....

Married on .... **at** ....

Other children .... **Born** ....

.... **Born** ....

.... **Born** ....

.... **Born** ....

Died on .... **at** ....

Buried on .... **at** ....

WIFE'S MATERNAL
PATERNAL GREAT-GRANDMOTHER 4

55 **Name** ....

Born on .... **at** ....

Educated ....

....

Qualifications ....

....

Career ....

....

Achievements ....

....

Addresses ....

....

Died on .... **at** ....

Buried on .... **at** ....

WIFE'S
3 MATERNAL GRANDFATHER

62

Name ....

Born on .... **at** ....

Educated ....

....

Qualifications ....

....

Career ....

....

Achievements ....

....

Addresses ....

....

Died on .... **at** ....

Buried on .... **at** ....

WIFE'S MATERNAL
MATERNAL GREAT-GRANDFATHER

Name ....

Born on .... **at** ....

Educated ....

....

Achievements/career ....

....

Married on .... **at** ....

....

Other children .... **Born** ....

.... **Born** ....

.... **Born** ....

.... **Born** ....

Died on .... **at** ....

Buried on .... **at** ....

WIFE'S MATERNAL
MATERNAL GREAT-GRANDMOTHER

Name ....

Born on .... **at** ....

Educated ....

....

Qualifications ....

....

Career ....

....

Achievements ....

....

Addresses ....

....

Died on .... **at** ....

Buried on .... **at** ....

WIFE'S
MATERNAL GRANDMOTHER

55

3

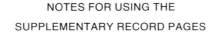

NOTES FOR USING THE
SUPPLEMENTARY RECORD PAGES

Pages 54-63 have dealt in detail with the researcher and spouse (generation 1), their parents (two each – generation 2), their grandparents (four each – generation 3), and their great-grandparents (eight each – generation 4).

The thirty-two pages that follow (66-97) are designed to enable you to follow back in the paternal line any of the great-grandparental (generation 4) families listed on pages 56-63.

For example, if having established the husband's paternal great-grandfather (generation 4), and having entered the particulars on page 56, you wish to extend his paternal line further backwards, you could use one or more of the supplementary pages (which contain two generations per page) as necessary, say pages 66-67. In the bottom left-hand box of page 67 you would include the details of the great-great-grandfather (generation 5), details of his wife in the bottom right-hand box and details of his parents in the top-left and right-hand boxes. In the same way, page 67 would then contain details of generations 7 and 8, and so on backwards.

Alternatively, or additionally, you could allocate pages to follow back the family of, say, the wife's maternal maternal great-grandmother (generation 4) on page 63 and so extend this family backwards.

The way the book is laid out is sufficiently flexible also to be used for following female descents, if so desired, by altering the bracketing in the centre of the supplementary pages so that the top two boxes relate to the bottom *right*-hand box (the wife's), rather than to the husband's as shown. In this way the female descent can be followed back generation by generation which could be helpful and interesting in cases of illegitimacy or where there is a descent in the female line, perhaps of names, resembl-ances, heirlooms, property or religion (e.g. Jewish).

Thus the supplementary pages provide the flexibility that is so important to the researcher, who is always at the mercy of available records, and where one branch of the family may be more interesting to research than another.

It is vital, however, to cross-reference these additional pages meticulously, both to and from the great-grandparents given on pages 56-63, as well as from one page to another. The small shield-shaped symbols at top and bottom should be used to denote the relevant cross-referenced page and the lozenges should indicate the generation number.

Pages 98 and 99 have been earmarked specifically to record details of any coats of arms that may have been used by different branches, with details of where, when and by whom registered. Pages 100-112 are allocated for details of family heirlooms, reunions, anecdotes, with a few pages for a scrapbook and notes.

Name ....

Born on .... **at** ....

Educated ....

....

Qualifications ....

....

Career ....

....

Achievements ....

....

Addresses ....

....

Died on .... **at** ....

Buried on .... **at** ....

Name ....

Born on .... **at** ....

Educated ....

....

Achievements/career ....

....

Married on .... **at** ....

Other children .... **Born** ....

.... **Born** ....

.... **Born** ....

.... **Born** ....

Died on .... **at** ....

Buried on .... **at** ....

Name ....

Born on .... **at** ....

Educated ....

....

Qualifications ....

....

Career ....

....

Achievements ....

....

Addresses ....

....

Died on .... **at** ....

Buried on .... **at** ....

Name ....

Born on .... **at** ....

Educated ....

....

Achievements/career ....

....

Married on .... **at** ....

Other children .... **Born** ....

.... **Born** ....

.... **Born** ....

.... **Born** ....

Died on .... **at** ....

Buried on .... **at** ....

Name ....

Born on .... **at** ....

Educated ....

....

Qualifications ....

....

Career ....

....

Achievements ....

....

Addresses ....

....

Died on .... **at** ....

Buried on .... **at** ....

Name ....

Born on .... **at** ....

Educated ....

....

Achievements/career ....

....

Married on .... **at** ....

....

Other children .... **Born** ....

.... **Born** ....

.... **Born** ....

.... **Born** ....

Died on .... **at** ....

Buried on .... **at** ....

Name ....

Born on .... **at** ....

Educated ....

....

Qualifications ....

....

Career ....

....

Achievements ....

....

Addresses ....

....

Died on .... **at** ....

Buried on .... **at** ....

Name ....

Born on .... **at** ....

Educated ....

....

Achievements/career ....

....

Married on .... **at** ....

....

Other children .... **Born** ....

.... **Born** ....

.... **Born** ....

.... **Born** ....

Died on .... **at** ....

Buried on .... **at** ....

Name ....

Born on .... **at** ....

Educated ....

....

Qualifications ....

....

Career ....

....

Achievements ....

....

Addresses ....

Died on .... **at** ....

Buried on .... **at** ....

Name ....

Born on .... **at** ....

Educated ....

....

Achievements/career ....

....

Married on .... **at** ....

Other children .... **Born** ....

.... **Born** ....

.... **Born** ....

.... **Born** ....

Died on .... **at** ....

Buried on .... **at** ....

Name ....

Born on .... **at** ....

Educated ....

....

Qualifications ....

....

Career ....

....

Achievements ....

....

Addresses ....

Died on .... **at** ....

Buried on .... **at** ....

Name ....

Born on .... **at** ....

Educated ....

....

Achievements/career ....

....

Married on .... **at** ....

Other children .... **Born** ....

.... **Born** ....

.... **Born** ....

.... **Born** ....

Died on .... **at** ....

Buried on .... **at** ....

Name ....

Born on .... **at** ....

Educated ....

....

Qualifications ....

....

Career ....

....

Achievements ....

....

Addresses ....

....

Died on .... **at** ....

Buried on .... **at** ....

Name ....

Born on .... **at** ....

Educated ....

....

Achievements/career ....

....

Married on .... **at** ....

....

Other children .... **Born** ....

.... **Born** ....

.... **Born** ....

.... **Born** ....

Died on .... **at** ....

Buried on .... **at** ....

Name ....

Born on .... **at** ....

Educated ....

....

Qualifications ....

....

Career ....

....

Achievements ....

....

Addresses ....

....

Died on .... **at** ....

Buried on .... **at** ....

Name ....

Born on .... **at** ....

Educated ....

....

Achievements/career ....

....

Married on .... **at** ....

....

Other children .... **Born** ....

.... **Born** ....

.... **Born** ....

.... **Born** ....

Died on .... **at** ....

Buried on .... **at** ....

Name ....

Born on .... at ....

Educated ....

....

Qualifications ....

....

Career ....

....

Achievements ....

....

Addresses ....

....

Died on .... at ....

Buried on .... at ....

Name ....

Born on .... at ....

Educated ....

Achievements/career ....

....

Married on .... at ....

Other children .... Born ....

.... Born ....

.... Born ....

.... Born ....

Died on .... at ....

Buried on .... at ....

Name ....

Born on .... at ....

Educated ....

....

Qualifications ....

....

Career ....

....

Achievements ....

....

Addresses ....

....

Died on .... at ....

Buried on .... at ....

Name ....

Born on .... at ....

Educated ....

Achievements/career ....

....

Married on .... at ....

Other children .... Born ....

.... Born ....

.... Born ....

.... Born ....

Died on .... at ....

Buried on .... at ....

Name ....

Born on .... **at** ....

Educated ....

....

Qualifications ....

....

Career ....

....

Achievements ....

....

Addresses ....

....

Died on .... **at** ....

Buried on .... **at** ....

Name ....

Born on .... **at** ....

Educated ....

....

Achievements/career ....

....

Married on .... **at** ....

....

Other children .... **Born** ......

.... **Born** ......

.... **Born** ......

.... **Born** ......

Died on .... **at** ....

Buried on .... **at** ....

Name ....

Born on .... **at** ....

Educated ....

....

Qualifications ....

....

Career ....

....

Achievements ....

....

Addresses ....

....

Died on .... **at** ....

Buried on .... **at** ....

Name ....

Born on .... **at** ....

Educated ....

....

Achievements/career ....

....

Married on .... **at** ....

....

Other children .... **Born** ......

.... **Born** ......

.... **Born** ......

.... **Born** ......

Died on .... **at** ....

Buried on .... **at** ....

Name ....

Born on .... **at** ....

Educated ....

....

Qualifications ....

....

Career ....

....

Achievements ....

....

Addresses ....

....

Died on .... **at** ....

Buried on .... **at** ....

Name ....

Born on .... **at** ....

Educated ....

....

Achievements/career ....

....

Married on .... **at** ....

....

Other children .... **Born** ....

.... **Born** ....

.... **Born** ....

.... **Born** ....

Died on .... **at** ....

Buried on .... **at** ....

Name ....

Born on .... **at** ....

Educated ....

....

Qualifications ....

....

Career ....

....

Achievements ....

....

Addresses ....

....

Died on .... **at** ....

Buried on .... **at** ....

Name ....

Born on .... **at** ....

Educated ....

....

Achievements/career ....

....

Married on .... **at** ....

....

Other children .... **Born** ....

.... **Born** ....

.... **Born** ....

.... **Born** ....

Died on .... **at** ....

Buried on .... **at** ....

Name ....

Born on .... **at** ....

Educated ....

....

Qualifications ....

....

Career ....

....

Achievements ....

....

Addresses ....

....

Died on .... **at** ....

Buried on .... **at** ....

Name ....

Born on .... **at** ....

Educated ....

....

Achievements/career ....

....

Married on .... **at** ....

....

Other children .... **Born** ....

.... **Born** ....

.... **Born** ....

.... **Born** ....

Died on .... **at** ....

Buried on .... **at** ....

Name ....

Born on .... **at** ....

Educated ....

....

Qualifications ....

....

Career ....

....

Achievements ....

....

Addresses ....

....

Died on .... **at** ....

Buried on .... **at** ....

Name ....

Born on .... **at** ....

Educated ....

....

Achievements/career ....

....

Married on .... **at** ....

....

Other children .... **Born** ....

.... **Born** ....

.... **Born** ....

.... **Born** ....

Died on .... **at** ....

Buried on .... **at** ....

Name ....

Born on .... **at** ....

Educated ....

....

Qualifications ....

....

Career ....

....

Achievements ....

....

Addresses ....

....

Died on .... **at** ....

Buried on .... **at** ....

Name ....

Born on .... **at** ....

Educated ....

....

Achievements/career ....

....

Married on .... **at** ....

....

Other children .... **Born** ....

.... **Born** ....

.... **Born** ....

.... **Born** ....

Died on .... **at** ....

Buried on .... **at** ....

Name ....

Born on .... **at** ....

Educated ....

....

Qualifications ....

....

Career ....

....

Achievements ....

....

Addresses ....

....

Died on .... **at** ....

Buried on .... **at** ....

Name ....

Born on .... **at** ....

Educated ....

....

Achievements/career ....

....

Married on .... **at** ....

....

Other children .... **Born** ....

.... **Born** ....

.... **Born** ....

.... **Born** ....

Died on .... **at** ....

Buried on .... **at** ....

Name ....

Born on .... **at** ....

Educated ....

....

Qualifications ....

....

Career ....

....

Achievements ....

....

Addresses ....

....

Died on .... **at** ....

Buried on .... **at** ....

Name ....

Born on .... **at** ....

Educated ....

....

Achievements/career ....

....

Married on .... **at** ....

....

Other children .... **Born** ....

.... **Born** ....

.... **Born** ....

.... **Born** ....

Died on .... **at** ....

Buried on .... **at** ....

Name ....

Born on .... **at** ....

Educated ....

....

Qualifications ....

....

Career ....

....

Achievements ....

....

Addresses ....

....

Died on .... **at** ....

Buried on .... **at** ....

Name ....

Born on .... **at** ....

Educated ....

....

Achievements/career ....

....

Married on .... **at** ....

....

Other children .... **Born** ....

.... **Born** ....

.... **Born** ....

.... **Born** ....

Died on .... **at** ....

Buried on .... **at** ....

Name ....

Born on .... **at** ....

Educated ....

....

Qualifications ....

....

Career ....

....

Achievements ....

....

Addresses ....

....

Died on .... **at** ....

Buried on .... **at** ....

Name ....

Born on .... **at** ....

Educated ....

....

Achievements/career ....

....

Married on .... **at** ....

....

Other children .... **Born** ....

.... **Born** ....

.... **Born** ....

.... **Born** ....

Died on .... **at** ....

Buried on .... **at** ....

Name ....

Born on .... **at** ....

Educated ....

....

Qualifications ....

....

Career ....

....

Achievements ....

....

Addresses ....

....

Died on .... **at** ....

Buried on .... **at** ....

Name ....

Born on .... **at** ....

Educated ....

....

Achievements/career ....

....

Married on .... **at** ....

....

Other children .... **Born** ....

.... **Born** ....

.... **Born** ....

.... **Born** ....

Died on .... **at** ....

Buried on .... **at** ....

FAMILY RECORDS

Name ....

Born on .... **at** ....

Educated ....
....

Qualifications ....
....

Career ....
....

Achievements ....
....

Addresses ....
....

Died on .... **at** ....

Buried on .... **at** ....

Name ....

Born on .... **at** ....

Educated ....
....

Achievements/career ....
....

Married on .... **at** ....

Other children .... **Born** ......
.... **Born** ......
.... **Born** ......
.... **Born** ......

Died on .... **at** ....

Buried on .... **at** ....

Name ....

Born on .... **at** ....

Educated ....
....

Qualifications ....
....

Career ....
....

Achievements ....
....

Addresses ....
....

Died on .... **at** ....

Buried on .... **at** ....

Name ....

Born on .... **at** ....

Educated ....
....

Achievements/career ....
....

Married on .... **at** ....

Other children .... **Born** ......
.... **Born** ......
.... **Born** ......
.... **Born** ......

Died on .... **at** ....

Buried on .... **at** ....

Name ....

Born on .... **at** ....

Educated ....

....

Qualifications ....

....

Career ....

....

Achievements ....

....

Addresses ....

....

Died on .... **at** ....

Buried on .... **at** ....

Name ....

Born on .... **at** ....

Educated ....

....

Achievements/career ....

....

Married on .... **at** ....

Other children .... **Born** ....

.... **Born** ....

.... **Born** ....

.... **Born** ....

Died on .... **at** ....

Buried on .... **at** ....

Name ....

Born on .... **at** ....

Educated ....

....

Qualifications ....

....

Career ....

....

Achievements ....

....

Addresses ....

....

Died on .... **at** ....

Buried on .... **at** ....

Name ....

Born on .... **at** ....

Educated ....

....

Achievements/career ....

....

Married on .... **at** ....

....

Other children .... **Born** ....

.... **Born** ....

.... **Born** ....

.... **Born** ....

Died on .... **at** ....

Buried on .... **at** ....

Name ....
Born on .... at ....
Educated ....
....
Qualifications ....
....
Career ....
....
Achievements ....
....
Addresses ....
....
Died on .... at ....
Buried on .... at ....

Name ....
Born on .... at ....
Educated ....
....
Achievements/career ....
....
Married on .... at ....
....
Other children .... Born ....
.... Born ....
.... Born ....
.... Born ....
Died on .... at ....
Buried on .... at ....

Name ....
Born on .... at ....
Educated ....
....
Qualifications ....
....
Career ....
....
Achievements ....
....
Addresses ....
....
Died on .... at ....
Buried on .... at ....

Name ....
Born on .... at ....
Educated ....
....
Achievements/career ....
....
Married on .... at ....
....
Other children .... Born ....
.... Born ....
.... Born ....
.... Born ....
Died on .... at ....
Buried on .... at ....

Name ....

Born on .... **at** ....

Educated ....

....

Qualifications ....

....

Career ....

....

Achievements ....

....

Addresses ....

....

Died on .... **at** ....

Buried on .... **at** ....

Name ....

Born on .... **at** ....

Educated ....

....

Achievements/career ....

....

Married on .... **at** ....

....

Other children .... **Born** ....

.... **Born** ....

.... **Born** ....

.... **Born** ....

Died on .... **at** ....

Buried on .... **at** ....

Name ....

Born on .... **at** ....

Educated ....

....

Qualifications ....

....

Career ....

....

Achievements ....

....

Addresses ....

....

Died on .... **at** ....

Buried on .... **at** ....

Name ....

Born on .... **at** ....

Educated ....

....

Achievements/career ....

....

Married on .... **at** ....

....

Other children .... **Born** ....

.... **Born** ....

.... **Born** ....

.... **Born** ....

Died on .... **at** ....

Buried on .... **at** ....

Name ....

Born on .... at ....

Educated ....

....

Qualifications ....

....

Career ....

....

Achievements ....

....

Addresses ....

....

Died on .... at ....

Buried on .... at ....

Name ....

Born on .... at ....

Educated ....

....

Achievements/career ....

....

Married on .... at ....

....

Other children .... Born ....

.... Born ....

.... Born ....

.... Born ....

Died on .... at ....

Buried on .... at ....

Name ....

Born on .... at ....

Educated ....

....

Qualifications ....

....

Career ....

....

Achievements ....

....

Addresses ....

....

Died on .... at ....

Buried on .... at ....

Name ....

Born on .... at ....

Educated ....

....

Achievements/career ....

....

Married on .... at ....

....

Other children .... Born ....

.... Born ....

.... Born ....

.... Born ....

Died on .... at ....

Buried on .... at ....

Name ....

Born on .... **at** ....

Educated ....

....

Qualifications ....

....

Career ....

....

Achievements ....

....

Addresses ....

....

Died on .... **at** ....

Buried on .... **at** ....

Name ....

Born on .... **at** ....

Educated ....

....

Achievements/career ....

....

Married on .... **at** ....

....

Other children .... **Born** ....

.... **Born** ....

.... **Born** ....

.... **Born** ....

Died on .... **at** ....

Buried on .... **at** ....

Name ....

Born on .... **at** ....

Educated ....

....

Qualifications ....

....

Career ....

....

Achievements ....

....

Addresses ....

....

Died on .... **at** ....

Buried on .... **at** ....

Name ....

Born on .... **at** ....

Educated ....

....

Achievements/career ....

....

Married on .... **at** ....

....

Other children .... **Born** ....

.... **Born** ....

.... **Born** ....

.... **Born** ....

Died on .... **at** ....

Buried on .... **at** ....

_____

Name ....

Born on .... at ....

Educated ....

....

Qualifications ....

....

Career ....

....

Achievements ....

....

Addresses ....

....

Died on .... at ....

Buried on .... at ....

Name ....

Born on .... at ....

Educated ....

....

Achievements/career ....

....

Married on .... at ....

....

Other children .... **Born** ....

.... **Born** ....

.... **Born** ....

.... **Born** ....

Died on .... at ....

Buried on .... at ....

_____   _____

Name ....

Born on .... at ....

Educated ....

....

Qualifications ....

....

Career ....

....

Achievements ....

....

Addresses ....

....

Died on .... at ....

Buried on .... at ....

Name ....

Born on .... at ....

Educated ....

....

Achievements/career ....

....

Married on .... at ....

....

Other children .... **Born** ....

.... **Born** ....

.... **Born** ....

.... **Born** ....

Died on .... at ....

Buried on .... at ....

_____   _____

Name ....

Born on .... **at** ....

Educated ....

....

Qualifications ....

....

Career ....

....

Achievements ....

....

Addresses ....

....

Died on .... **at** ....

Buried on .... **at** ....

Name ....

Born on .... **at** ....

Educated ....

....

Achievements/career ....

....

Married on .... **at** ....

Other children .... **Born** ....

.... **Born** ....

.... **Born** ....

.... **Born** ....

Died on .... **at** ....

Buried on .... **at** ....

Name ....

Born on .... **at** ....

Educated ....

....

Qualifications ....

....

Career ....

....

Achievements ....

....

Addresses ....

....

Died on .... **at** ....

Buried on .... **at** ....

Name ....

Born on .... **at** ....

Educated ....

....

Achievements/career ....

....

Married on .... **at** ....

Other children .... **Born** ....

.... **Born** ....

.... **Born** ....

.... **Born** ....

Died on .... **at** ....

Buried on .... **at** ....

Name ....

Born on .... **at** ....

Educated ....

....

Qualifications ....

....

Career ....

....

Achievements ....

....

Addresses ....

....

Died on .... **at** ....

Buried on .... **at** ....

Name ....

Born on .... **at** ....

Educated ....

....

Achievements/career ....

....

Married on .... **at** ....

....

Other children .... **Born** ....

.... **Born** ....

.... **Born** ....

.... **Born** ....

Died on .... **at** ....

Buried on .... **at** ....

Name ....

Born on .... **at** ....

Educated ....

....

Qualifications ....

....

Career ....

....

Achievements ....

....

Addresses ....

....

Died on .... **at** ....

Buried on .... **at** ....

Name ....

Born on .... **at** ....

Educated ....

....

Achievements/career ....

....

Married on .... **at** ....

....

Other children .... **Born** ....

.... **Born** ....

.... **Born** ....

.... **Born** ....

Died on .... **at** ....

Buried on .... **at** ....

Name ....

Born on .... **at** ....

Educated ....

....

Qualifications ....

....

Career ....

....

Achievements ....

....

Addresses ....

....

Died on .... **at** ....

Buried on .... **at** ....

Name ....

Born on .... **at** ....

Educated ....

....

Achievements/career ....

....

Married on .... **at** ....

Other children .... **Born** ....

.... **Born** ....

.... **Born** ....

.... **Born** ....

Died on .... **at** ....

Buried on .... **at** ....

Name ....

Born on .... **at** ....

Educated ....

....

Qualifications ....

....

Career ....

....

Achievements ....

....

Addresses ....

....

Died on .... **at** ....

Buried on .... **at** ....

Name ....

Born on .... **at** ....

Educated ....

....

Achievements/career ....

....

Married on .... **at** ....

Other children .... **Born** ....

.... **Born** ....

.... **Born** ....

.... **Born** ....

Died on .... **at** ....

Buried on .... **at** ....

Name ....

Born on .... **at** ....

Educated ....

....

Qualifications ....

....

Career ....

....

Achievements ....

....

Addresses ....

....

Died on .... **at** ....

Buried on .... **at** ....

Name ....

Born on .... **at** ....

Educated ....

....

Achievements/career ....

....

Married on .... **at** ....

....

Other children .... **Born** ....

.... **Born** ....

.... **Born** ....

.... **Born** ....

Died on .... **at** ....

Buried on .... **at** ....

Name ....

Born on .... **at** ....

Educated ....

....

Qualifications ....

....

Career ....

....

Achievements ....

....

Addresses ....

....

Died on .... **at** ....

Buried on .... **at** ....

Name ....

Born on .... **at** ....

Educated ....

....

Achievements/career ....

....

Married on .... **at** ....

....

Other children .... **Born** ....

.... **Born** ....

.... **Born** ....

.... **Born** ....

Died on .... **at** ....

Buried on .... **at** ....

Name ....

Born on .... **at** ....

Educated ....

....

Qualifications ....

....

Career ....

....

Achievements ....

....

Addresses ....

....

Died on .... **at** ....

Buried on .... **at** ....

Name ....

Born on .... **at** ....

Educated ....

....

Achievements/career ....

....

Married on .... **at** ....

....

Other children .... **Born** ....

.... **Born** ....

.... **Born** ....

.... **Born** ....

Died on .... **at** ....

Buried on .... **at** ....

Name ....

Born on .... **at** ....

Educated ....

....

Qualifications ....

....

Career ....

....

Achievements ....

....

Addresses ....

....

Died on .... **at** ....

Buried on .... **at** ....

Name ....

Born on .... **at** ....

Educated ....

....

Achievements/career ....

....

Married on .... **at** ....

....

Other children .... **Born** ....

.... **Born** ....

.... **Born** ....

.... **Born** ....

Died on .... **at** ....

Buried on .... **at** ....

Name ....

Born on .... **at** ....

Educated ....

....

Qualifications ....

....

Career ....

....

Achievements ....

....

Addresses ....

....

Died on .... **at** ....

Buried on .... **at** ....

Name ....

Born on .... **at** ....

Educated ....

....

Achievements/career ....

....

Married on .... **at** ....

....

Other children .... **Born** ....

.... **Born** ....

.... **Born** ....

.... **Born** ....

Died on .... **at** ....

Buried on .... **at** ....

Name ....

Born on .... **at** ....

Educated ....

....

Qualifications ....

....

Career ....

....

Achievements ....

....

Addresses ....

....

Died on .... **at** ....

Buried on .... **at** ....

Name ....

Born on .... **at** ....

Educated ....

....

Achievements/career ....

....

Married on .... **at** ....

....

Other children .... **Born** ....

.... **Born** ....

.... **Born** ....

.... **Born** ....

Died on .... **at** ....

Buried on .... **at** ....

Name ....

Born on .... **at** ....

Educated ....

....

Qualifications ....

....

Career ....

....

Achievements ....

....

Addresses ....

....

Died on .... **at** ....

Buried on .... **at** ....

Name ....

Born on .... **at** ....

Educated ....

....

Achievements/career ....

....

Married on .... **at** ....

....

Other children .... **Born** ....

.... **Born** ....

.... **Born** ....

.... **Born** ....

Died on .... **at** ....

Buried on .... **at** ....

Name ....

Born on .... **at** ....

Educated ....

....

Qualifications ....

....

Career ....

....

Achievements ....

....

Addresses ....

....

Died on .... **at** ....

Buried on .... **at** ....

Name ....

Born on .... **at** ....

Educated ....

....

Achievements/career ....

....

Married on .... **at** ....

....

Other children .... **Born** ....

.... **Born** ....

.... **Born** ....

.... **Born** ....

Died on .... **at** ....

Buried on .... **at** ....

Name ....

Born on .... **at** ....

Educated ....

....

Qualifications ....

....

Career ....

....

Achievements ....

....

Addresses ....

....

Died on .... **at** ....

Buried on .... **at** ....

Name ....

Born on .... **at** ....

Educated ....

....

Achievements/career ....

....

Married on .... **at** ....

....

Other children .... **Born** ....

.... **Born** ....

.... **Born** ....

.... **Born** ....

Died on .... **at** ....

Buried on .... **at** ....

Name ....

Born on .... **at** ....

Educated ....

....

Qualifications ....

....

Career ....

....

Achievements ....

....

Addresses ....

....

Died on .... **at** ....

Buried on .... **at** ....

Name ....

Born on .... **at** ....

Educated ....

....

Achievements/career ....

....

Married on .... **at** ....

....

Other children .... **Born** ....

.... **Born** ....

.... **Born** ....

.... **Born** ....

Died on .... **at** ....

Buried on .... **at** ....

Name ....

Born on .... **at** ....

Educated ....

....

Qualifications ....

....

Career ....

....

Achievements ....

....

Addresses ....

....

Died on .... **at** ....

Buried on .... **at** ....

Name ....

Born on .... **at** ....

Educated ....

....

Achievements/career ....

....

Married on .... **at** ....

Other children .... **Born** ....

.... **Born** ....

.... **Born** ....

.... **Born** ....

Died on .... **at** ....

Buried on .... **at** ....

Name ....

Born on .... **at** ....

Educated ....

....

Qualifications ....

....

Career ....

....

Achievements ....

....

Addresses ....

....

Died on .... **at** ....

Buried on .... **at** ....

Name ....

Born on .... **at** ....

Educated ....

....

Achievements/career ....

....

Married on .... **at** ....

....

Other children .... **Born** ....

.... **Born** ....

.... **Born** ....

.... **Born** ....

Died on .... **at** ....

Buried on .... **at** ....

FAMILY RECORDS

Name ....

Born on .... **at** ....

Educated ....
....

Qualifications ....
....

Career ....
....

Achievements ....
....

Addresses ....
....

Died on .... **at** ....

Buried on .... **at** ....

Name ....

Born on .... **at** ....

Educated ....
....

Achievements/career ....
....

Married on .... **at** ....
....

Other children .... **Born** ....
.... **Born** ....
.... **Born** ....
.... **Born** ....

Died on .... **at** ....

Buried on .... **at** ....

Name ....

Born on .... **at** ....

Educated ....
....

Qualifications ....
....

Career ....
....

Achievements ....
....

Addresses ....
....

Died on .... **at** ....

Buried on .... **at** ....

Name ....

Born on .... **at** ....

Educated ....
....

Achievements/career ....
....

Married on .... **at** ....
....

Other children .... **Born** ....
.... **Born** ....
.... **Born** ....
.... **Born** ....

Died on .... **at** ....

Buried on .... **at** ....

93

FAMILY RECORDS

Name ....

Born on .... **at** ....

Educated ....

....

Qualifications ....

....

Career ....

....

Achievements ....

....

Addresses ....

....

Died on .... **at** ....

Buried on .... **at** ....

Name ....

Born on .... **at** ....

Educated ....

....

Achievements/career ....

....

Married on .... **at** ....

Other children .... **Born** ....

.... **Born** ....

.... **Born** ....

.... **Born** ....

Died on .... **at** ....

Buried on .... **at** ....

Name ....

Born on .... **at** ....

Educated ....

....

Qualifications ....

....

Career ....

....

Achievements ....

....

Addresses ....

....

Died on .... **at** ....

Buried on .... **at** ....

Name ....

Born on .... **at** ....

Educated ....

....

Achievements/career ....

....

Married on .... **at** ....

Other children .... **Born** ....

.... **Born** ....

.... **Born** ....

.... **Born** ....

Died on .... **at** ....

Buried on .... **at** ....

Name ....

Born on .... **at** ....

Educated ....

....

Qualifications ....

....

Career ....

....

Achievements ....

....

Addresses ....

....

Died on .... **at** ....

Buried on .... **at** ....

Name ....

Born on .... **at** ....

Educated ....

....

Achievements/career ....

....

Married on .... **at** ....

....

Other children .... **Born** ....

.... **Born** ....

.... **Born** ....

.... **Born** ....

Died on .... **at** ....

Buried on .... **at** ....

Name ....

Born on .... **at** ....

Educated ....

....

Qualifications ....

....

Career ....

....

Achievements ....

....

Addresses ....

....

Died on .... **at** ....

Buried on .... **at** ....

Name ....

Born on .... **at** ....

Educated ....

....

Achievements/career ....

....

Married on .... **at** ....

....

Other children .... **Born** ....

.... **Born** ....

.... **Born** ....

.... **Born** ....

Died on .... **at** ....

Buried on .... **at** ....

Name ....

Born on .... **at** ....

Educated ....

....

Qualifications ....

....

Career ....

....

Achievements ....

....

Addresses ....

....

Died on .... **at** ....

Buried on .... **at** ....

Name ....

Born on .... **at** ....

Educated ....

....

Achievements/career ....

....

Married on .... **at** ....

....

Other children .... **Born** ....

.... **Born** ....

.... **Born** ....

.... **Born** ....

Died on .... **at** ....

Buried on .... **at** ....

Name ....

Born on .... **at** ....

Educated ....

....

Qualifications ....

....

Career ....

....

Achievements ....

....

Addresses ....

....

Died on .... **at** ....

Buried on .... **at** ....

Name ....

Born on .... **at** ....

Educated ....

....

Achievements/career ....

....

Married on .... **at** ....

....

Other children .... **Born** ....

.... **Born** ....

.... **Born** ....

.... **Born** ....

Died on .... **at** ....

Buried on .... **at** ....

Name ....

Born on .... at ....

Educated ....

....

Qualifications ....

....

Career ....

....

Achievements ....

....

Addresses ....

....

Died on .... at ....

Buried on .... at ....

Name ....

Born on .... at ....

Educated ....

....

Achievements/career ....

....

Married on .... at ....

....

Other children .... Born ....

.... Born ....

.... Born ....

.... Born ....

Died on .... at ....

Buried on .... at ....

Name ....

Born on .... at ....

Educated ....

....

Qualifications ....

....

Career ....

....

Achievements ....

....

Addresses ....

....

Died on .... at ....

Buried on .... at ....

Name ....

Born on .... at ....

Educated ....

....

Achievements/career ....

....

Married on .... at ....

....

Other children .... Born ....

.... Born ....

.... Born ....

.... Born ....

Died on .... at ....

Buried on .... at ....

Name ....

Registered at ....

On .... **Reference** ....

Name ....

Registered at ....

On .... **Reference** ....

Name ....

Registered at ....

On .... **Reference** ....

Name ....

Registered at ....

On .... **Reference** ....

Name ....

Registered at ....

On .... **Reference** ....

Name ....

Registered at ....

On .... **Reference** ....

Name ....

Registered at ....

On .... **Reference** ....

Name ....

Registered at ....

On .... **Reference** ....

HEIRLOOMS

HEIRLOOMS

....

....

....

....

....

....

....

....

....

....

....

....

....

....

....

ANECDOTES

ANECDOTES

ANECDOTES

ANECDOTES

SCRAPBOOK

SCRAPBOOK

SCRAPBOOK

SCRAPBOOK

NOTES